Neighborhood & Community Write & Read Books

BY CATHERINE M. TAMBLYN

What Is in a Neighborhood?

by _____

A City Walk

by _____

Meet Community Helpers

by _____

New York • Toronto • London • Auckland • Sydney
Mexico City • New Delhi • Hong Kong • Buenos Aires

Teaching Resources

To Biz—my very best friend.

Cover design by Lillian Kohli

Cover and interior illustrations by Maxie Chambliss

Interior design by Ellen Matlach for Boultinghouse & Boultinghouse

ISBN-13: 978-0-439-49160-0

ISBN-10: 0-439-49160-6

Copyright © 2006 by Catherine M. Tamblyn

Published by Scholastic Inc.

3 4 5 6 7 8 9 10   40   14 13 12 11 10 09 08

Contents

Neighborhood & Community Write & Read Books

Neighborhoods & Communities

People in the Community

Maps & Geography

Introduction

Neighborhood & Community Write & Read Books are an engaging way to build reading and writing skills while learning about social studies topics such as homes, jobs, transportation, mapping, and different types of communities. Each book features predictable text that children complete. Some books invite children to draw illustrations. When finished, children will have their own personalized books that they'll be motivated to read again and again.

Since these books correlate to common social studies themes, they are easy to integrate into the curriculum. On pages 7–16, you'll find suggestions for introducing the books and making them, as well as ideas for extending learning. The books are also easy enough for children to assemble. Assembly directions appear on page 5.

Children will be proud to share their one-of-a-kind books at home and in school. Rereading the books and sharing them with others reinforces the concepts covered. Providing children with opportunities to read aloud also helps them develop fluency. Children will enjoy sharing their books as much as they enjoyed creating them, and they'll build skills and content knowledge in the process. Enjoy!

Connections to the Standards

These books are designed to support you in meeting the following reading, writing, and geography standards outlined by Mid-continent Research for Education and Learning (McREL), an organization that collects and synthesizes national and state standards.

Reading
- Uses the general skills and strategies of the reading process.
- Uses reading skills and strategies to understand and interpret a variety of informational texts.

Writing
- Uses the general skills and strategies of the writing process.
- Uses grammatical and mechanical conventions in written compositions.
- Uses the stylistic and rhetorical aspects of writing.

Geography
- Understands the characteristics and uses of maps, globes, and other geographic tools and technologies.
- Knows the location of places, geographic features, and patterns of the environment.
- Knows the location of school, home, neighborhood, community, state, and country.
- Understands the physical and human characteristics of place.
- Knows the physical and human characteristics of the local community (e.g., neighborhoods, schools, parks, creeks, shopping areas, and so on).
- Knows that places can be defined in terms of their predominant human and physical characteristics (e.g., rural, urban, forest, desert, and so on).

Source: *Content Knowledge: A Compendium of Standards and Benchmarks for K–12 Education* (4th ed.). Mid-continent Research for Education and Learning, 2006.

Getting Started With Write & Read Books

These books are designed for flexible use. Below are suggested guidelines for using the books in the classroom. Feel free to adapt any ideas to better meet the needs of your students.

Introducing the Books

Prior to having children create their books, it is helpful to introduce the social studies concepts to children, build background knowledge on the topics, and preteach any vocabulary words they will encounter in the text. It is a good idea to create a sample book in advance and read it aloud to children, pointing out the text and illustrations that you added to the book. This process will help children feel more confident when they create their own books.

Making the Books

The amount of guidance required as children work on their books will depend on their individual needs. If children need more support, create the books as a small-group or whole-class activity, having children complete a few pages at a time. You might work together to brainstorm possible responses for each page and record these on chart paper. Children can refer to the chart as they are writing. If students need additional support, you might have them dictate the text and then write it in dotted-line letters for them to trace.

Sharing the Books

Once children have finished the books, encourage them to read their books to themselves and provide opportunities for them to share their work with others. You might have children share their books with partners, with small groups, or with the whole class. To give everyone a chance to share, ask children to choose a page from their book to read to the whole class. Invite students to discuss their illustrations as well. Encourage students to ask questions and provide positive feedback about one another's work. Be sure to send the books home for children to share with their families. A letter is provided on page 6 to introduce Write & Read Books to families. A reproducible "About the Author" template appears on page 96.

Assembling the Books

Provide children with copies of the reproducible book pages and demonstrate the steps below. Or you might assemble the books in advance.

1. Carefully remove the perforated pages from the book. Make single-sided copies on standard 8½-inch by 11-inch paper.

2. Fold the front cover/back cover in half along the dotted line, keeping the fold to the left side.

3. Fold each interior page in half, keeping the fold to the right side.

4. Place the interior pages inside the cover and staple three times along the spine.

_____
                          Date

Dear Family,

Our class is making books that cover social studies topics and help children build reading and writing skills. These books include predictable text that is easy to read. They cover key topics such as homes, neighborhoods, communities, jobs, transportation, and mapping.

Each student adds writing and illustrations to complete the books and personalize them. The children are proud of their work and are eager to share it with you. We hope that you'll enjoy reading these books together. When reading the books, I encourage you to ask questions about the text or illustrations and provide positive feedback about your child's ideas, illustrations, handwriting, or overall presentation. You might also comment on your child's reading expression and fluency.

Thank you very much for your participation. Your encouragement will mean a great deal to your child.

Sincerely,

_____

Teaching Ideas

Home, Sweet Home
pages 17–22

Purpose
Children learn about different types of homes.

Strategies for Starting
Ask children what a home is and why people need homes, such as to provide protection, shelter, warmth, coolness, safety, storage for belongings, a place to sleep, and so on. Discuss the variety of homes in which people live, including apartments, mobile homes, houseboats, cabins, town houses, houses, shelters, senior residences, and so on. Note the types of homes that are found in children's own community.

Introduce the Book
In advance, prepare a book as a model. Read the sample book aloud to children and encourage them to fill in the blanks. Discuss different responses for page 1. Pause to review the variety of homes on page 2. Encourage children to suggest additional types of homes.

Make the Book
Distribute copies of the reproducible book pages and assist children as they assemble their own books. As an alternative, provide children with preassembled books. As children make their books, suggest that they use the picture clues to determine how to complete the text.

Share the Book
Have children share their books with partners. Encourage them to respond to their partner's work with thoughtful questions and positive comments. Invite children to share their responses on pages 1 and 10 with the class.

Beyond the Book
- Examine photographs of homes throughout the world. Compare and contrast homes and create an adjectives word chart to describe the materials, shape, or function of the homes.
- Discuss materials used in home construction and relate them to climate and the availability of natural resources.
- Use paper lunch bags to create an assortment of three-dimensional homes. Stuff the bags with tissue paper. Fold down the tops of the bags and decorate with cut paper or drawings to make different types of homes.

What Is in a Neighborhood?
pages 23–27

Purpose
Children learn about some of the common features of neighborhoods.

Strategies for Starting
Invite children to describe their neighborhoods. Record their responses on chart paper. Then work together to compile a list of what these places have in common: streets, homes, and people living in them. Discuss other features neighborhoods might have, such as playgrounds, schools, stores, and so on. Explain that neighborhoods are different from one another and may have different types of places in them—for instance, some neighborhoods have stores while others have only homes.

Introduce the Book
In advance, prepare a book as a model. Read your book aloud to children. Point out that your responses reflect places in your own neighborhood. Remind children that their responses will be different. Point out that your illustrations match the text.

Make the Book

Distribute copies of the reproducible book pages and assist children as they assemble their own books. As an alternative, provide children with preassembled books. Explain that children will write about their own neighborhood and draw illustrations to match the text.

Share the Book

Encourage children to share their books with the class. You may want to display a map of the community. After each presentation, point out the neighborhoods named in their books.

Beyond the Book

- Display a map of the children's community. Point out the different neighborhoods within the community.
- Build a three-dimensional model of a neighborhood on mural paper, using the lunch-bag homes. (See Home, Sweet Home on page 7.) Use a marker to draw streets, parks, and other features on the mural paper.

Communities Big and Small

pages 28–34

Communities Big and Small

by _____

Purpose

Children learn about urban, suburban, and rural communities and their features.

Strategies for Starting

Discuss the meaning of the word *community*. After students have shared several ideas, explain that the word *community* has different meanings. Share the definition of a community as a group of neighborhoods, providing examples of neighborhoods that students may know from their own experience. Share other definitions as well, such as classroom community, and ask children what it means to belong to a community.

Introduce the Book

In advance, prepare a book as a model. Read your book aloud to children. Pause to discuss possible responses for pages 2 and 3, such as *live, play, work, learn,* and *shop*. Note that all communities have similar features yet they are all different in terms of people, places, size, and location.

Make the Book

Distribute copies of the reproducible book pages and assist children as they assemble their own books. As an alternative, provide children with preassembled books. As children make their books, suggest that they use the picture clues to determine how to complete the text.

Share the Book

Have children share their books with a partner, taking turns reading each page. Children can compare their answers and discuss any differences. As a group, discuss the different features of the types of communities mentioned in the book. Then work together to make a tally chart of the communities children would like to visit (on page 11). Invite volunteers to share the reasons that support their choices.

Beyond the Book

- Trace the outline of children's communities on a map.
- Have children identify different types of communities mentioned in the fiction and nonfiction books they are reading.
- Join the three-dimensional neighborhoods previously created with stuffed paper lunch bags (see What Is in a Neighborhood?, left) to create a community.

Postcards From the Country

pages 35–39

Postcards From the Country

Dear Grandma,
We are having a wonderful time!

by _____

Purpose

Children learn about a variety of environments in rural areas, such as deserts, forests, and farms.

Strategies for Starting

Discuss the meaning of the word *country*. Explain that the word can mean a nation such as the United States of America. Trace the United States on a map or globe. Explain that the word *country* also means natural areas outside of cities and suburbs. Ask children what things they might expect to see in the country, and compile a list. Show photographs of different country settings, including those mentioned in the book. Preteach vocabulary words children will encounter in the text, such as *ranch, orchard, desert,* and *forest.*

Introduce the Book

In advance, prepare a book as a model. Before reading the text, show students that you have illustrated a postcard on each page showing a different country environment. Ask children why people send postcards from places they visit. Provide examples of real postcards for children to examine. Redirect children's attention to the book and explain that the words below each illustration are a message from the sender of the postcard. Read and discuss each postcard.

Make the Book

Distribute copies of the reproducible book pages and assist children as they assemble their own books. As an alternative, provide children with preassembled books. Explain that children will add details to each message and then draw a picture of the front of the postcard to illustrate the text. Tell children that there are many possible ways to complete the text on each page. On the last page, children choose a place in the country to write about and draw, such as a lake, beach, or canyon.

Share the Book

Encourage children to share their postcards with small groups and the class. Note the variety of messages and details in the pictures.

Beyond the Book

• Create a bulletin board display showing different pages from children's completed books. Add real postcards to the display that show other places in the countryside.

• Make a collage of magazine pictures showing different country settings. Include words that describe the pictures as well as words that express emotions or feelings evoked by the pictures.

• Display and share items bought or gathered from country places.

A City Walk

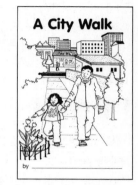

pages 40–44

Purpose

Children learn about the features of cities.

Strategies for Starting

If children live in rural or suburban areas, ask them if they have ever visited a city. On chart paper, record different things that students have seen in cities or think they might see in cities, such as stores, restaurants, apartment buildings, skyscrapers, museums, parks, schools, fire stations, cars, taxis, subways, and buses.

Introduce the Book

In advance, prepare a book as a model. Ask students to imagine that they are visiting a city and taking pictures of all the different things they see. Read aloud the book, pausing to let students fill in the blanks using the pictures you drew as clues.

Make the Book

Distribute copies of the reproducible book pages and assist children as they assemble their own books. As an alternative, provide children with preassembled books. Invite children to fill in the blanks on each page using the clues in the text. Then have them draw an illustration to match the text.

Share the Book

Have children share their book with a partner and compare their drawings of each place. Invite children to share their responses on pages 7 and 8. Make a bar graph showing the places students would most like to visit in a city.

Beyond the Book

- Create a book corner with fiction and nonfiction books about cities. Include books that show cities all over the world.
- Have students draw postcards from cities they have visited or researched. On the back, invite students to write something they know about these cities.
- Invite students to work together to create a city with blocks or recyclable materials, such as empty cereal boxes and paper towel tubes.

I Travel

pages 45–49

Purpose

Children explore different kinds of transportation on land, on water, and in the air.

Strategies for Starting

Invite children to name different ways to travel from place to place. Responses may include a bicycle, skateboard, scooter, wheelchair, feet, horse, bus, plane, train, and subway. Ask children how people choose their mode of transportation. Some factors might include how far they are going, how quickly they need to get there, what resources are available, and so on. Invite volunteers to share their own experiences taking various forms of transportation.

Introduce the Book

In advance, prepare a book as a model. Read your book aloud to children. Encourage children to fill in the blanks using the pictures as clues. Preteach vocabulary words as needed.

Make the Book

Distribute copies of the reproducible book pages and assist children as they assemble their own books. As an alternative, provide children with preassembled books. Explain that students will fill in the blanks using the pictures and text as clues.

Share the Book

Invite volunteers to read their books aloud to a group or to the class. Encourage students to ask thoughtful questions and provide positive feedback. Add the books to a reading corner with additional books about transportation.

Beyond the Book

- Play a transportation name game by making transportation-related sounds and pantomiming different forms of transportation for children to identify. Invite children to take turns acting out different vehicles.
- Make three murals or collages showing different vehicles that travel by air, water, and land.
- Discuss ways people can travel safely, such as by using seatbelts, bicycle helmets, reflectors, and bike lanes. Create a bulletin board about travel safety.

Community Signs

pages 50–55

Purpose

Children identify different signs and learn what information they provide.

Strategies for Starting

Talk about signs in your classroom and examine their purpose. Ask children where else they see signs and what purpose these signs serve. Point out that some signs use words while others use pictures. Some signs use both words and pictures. Discuss why picture signs might be helpful to more people (such as young children who are learning to read, people who have difficulty reading, or people who speak languages other than English).

Introduce the Book

In advance, prepare a book as a model. Display the cover and ask a volunteer to identify the recycling symbol sign. Ask what the symbol means and what it tells the child on the cover to do. Ask children

where else they have seen the recycling sign in their community. Explain that this book is about a variety of community signs and about the many ways these signs can help them. As you read, encourage children to fill in the blanks.

Make the Book
Distribute copies of the reproducible book pages and assist children as they assemble their own books. As an alternative, provide children with preassembled books. Have students use the picture clues to fill in the missing words.

Share the Book
Have children read their completed books in pairs, taking turns reading each page. Encourage them to compare their answers and discuss any differences.

Beyond the Book
• Take a walking tour of the school neighborhood and note the variety of signs found. Discuss their distinctive shapes and the information they provide. Then have children create a scrapbook, tally chart, or graph of their findings.
• Explore signs that are found in communities outside of school.
• Examine a variety of maps to find picture symbols that are also found on community signs.

My Very Own Community
pages 56–61
Purpose
Children create a book about their own community.

Strategies for Starting
Review the definition of a community. Ask children to name places in their community and compile a list, such as places to shop, play, learn, work, and eat. Have children name features of their community such as types of homes, landforms or bodies of water, community workers, and types of transportation. Discuss how people

entertain themselves in children's communities, such as by holding block parties, festivals, parades, or other events.

Introduce the Book
In advance, prepare a book as a model. If your community is different from your students' communities, share its location on a local map prior to reading your book aloud. Point out that your book will be different from the books students will make because all communities are different. Tell children that they will make books about their own communities.

Make the Book
Distribute copies of the reproducible book pages and assist children as they assemble their own books. As an alternative, provide children with preassembled books. Explain that children will draw themselves on the cover and fill in the name of their community. (You may need to provide the correct spelling.) Help children identify the type of community it is: city, suburb, town, or rural community. On page 2, children describe the land in their community and name a body of water in it or nearby. Display a local map to help children find this information. Have children draw illustrations to match the text throughout the rest of the book.

Share the Book
Provide opportunities for children to share their completed books with small groups or with the class. Note the variety of answers given. Encourage children to ask questions about their classmates' books and provide positive feedback.

Beyond the Book
• Locate children's communities on a map.
• Make an oversized map of children's communities, including the places named in their books.
• Turn children's books into scripts to create a read-aloud play about their communities. Replace the word *my* with *our* throughout. Allow different children to present each page. Conclude the play with children naming the best things about their communities.

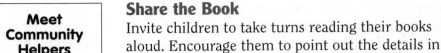

Meet Community Helpers

pages 62–66

Purpose
Children learn about community workers who provide services.

Strategies for Starting
To introduce the concept of providing a service, ask children to describe things their caregivers do to help them. Responses might include providing rides to and from school, helping with homework, washing clothes, and making meals. Explain that when their caregivers help them, they are providing a service. Invite children to name services or jobs that they do at home or school to help others. Tell children that they will be making a book about community workers who help others by providing services as part of their jobs. Ask children to name several community helpers while you record their responses on chart paper. Discuss why these jobs are important.

Introduce the Book
In advance, prepare a book as a model. Read your book aloud to children. Pause throughout the book to ask children what else each community helper does to assist people. Point out the details you included in each illustration, such as tools, vehicles, or uniforms.

Make the Book
Distribute copies of the reproducible book pages and assist children as they assemble their own books. As an alternative, provide children with preassembled books. Instruct children to add information on each page about the featured community helper. Then have children draw an illustration to match the text. Suggest that they also add details to each picture, such as tools, vehicles, or other objects related to the job. Explain that on page 8 they will write about a community helper that has not been mentioned in the book.

Share the Book
Invite children to take turns reading their books aloud. Encourage them to point out the details in their illustrations and share information about the community helper they wrote about on page 8.

Beyond the Book
- Have children interview your school crossing guard, librarian, custodian, and other community helpers about their jobs.
- Design a "Workers Wall of Fame" by displaying page 8 of each child's book.
- Invite children to research and share information about the job they might like to do when they grow up.

TEACHING TIP: Have children create these books around Labor Day.

What Do They Do?

pages 67–70

Purpose
Children learn about community workers who produce or grow goods.

Strategies for Starting
Ask children what things caregivers might make for them, such as meals, snacks, clothes, blankets, toys, and so on. Invite children to name things they make for others—for example, paintings, pictures, cards, and crafts. Tell children that they will be making a book about community workers who make or grow things. Explain that these things are called goods. Begin by making a list of workers, such as a pastry chef, bicycle builder, artist, or jewelry designer. Ask children to identify the good that each person makes.

Introduce the Book
In advance, prepare a book as a model. On each page, invite a volunteer to read the question about

the worker. Then read aloud the worker's response. Pause at each blank to allow children to name the missing word.

Make the Book
Distribute copies of the reproducible book pages and assist children as they assemble their own books. As an alternative, provide children with preassembled books. Explain to children that they will draw a good that each person might make and then fill in the blank with the name of the good.

Share the Book
Have children read their books in pairs, with one child reading the question for the worker and the other child reading the worker's response. Invite children to pantomime the worker's actions as they are reading the workers' responses. You might provide props such as hats and play tools for students to wear or use as they read.

Beyond the Book
• Discuss the skills needed to do each job mentioned in the book.
• Explore tools, utensils, and machines used by workers who make goods.
• Create a matching game with labeled cards that feature goods and the workers who make them. Have students play a game of concentration to match the pairs of cards.

TEACHING TIP: Have children create these books around Labor Day.

From Farm to Me
pages 71–75
Purpose
Children learn about the process of growing a vegetable crop.

Strategies for Starting
Have children brainstorm words related to farms, such as *farmers, animals, farm equipment, machines, buildings, irrigation,* and *crops.* Provide

From Farm to Me

opportunities for children to share their knowledge of farms from personal experiences visiting farms, from reading, or from other sources. Discuss some of the products that come from farms, including fruits and vegetables. Preteach vocabulary words in the text as needed.

Introduce the Book
In advance, prepare a book as a model. Read your book aloud to children. Point out that each picture illustrates one step in a process. After reading, challenge children to recall the steps.

Make the Book
Distribute copies of the reproducible book pages and assist children as they assemble their own books. As an alternative, provide children with preassembled books. Explain to children that they will fill in the missing text, using the pictures as clues.

Share the Book
Have children share their completed books in pairs, taking turns reading each page. Invite children to share their responses on page 8 with the class. Make a class graph or chart showing children's favorite fruits and vegetables. As an alternative, have students create a collaborative banner with drawings of their favorite fruits and vegetables.

Beyond the Book
• Make a linear display of the steps in the process by clipping the book pages in order on a clothesline. Add pictures and text for additional steps such as purchasing the vegetables, bringing them home, cooking them, and eating them.
• Cut apart the pages, cover the number on each page, and place the pages out of order. Invite children to put the pictures back in order to show the process.
• Grow seeds in cups. Have children write and illustrate the steps in the process.
• Have children role-play the process described in the book.

I Am a Good Citizen

pages 76–80

Purpose

Children write and draw to show aspects of good citizenship.

Strategies for Starting

Invite children to name things they do that make them good classmates. Record their responses on chart paper. Some possible responses are sharing, caring, being helpful, working together, being respectful and fair, obeying class rules, listening, and putting away materials. Point out that these actions are part of classroom citizenship. Ask children what might happen if students did not do these things. Possible responses might include that the classroom would become messy, it would be hard to learn, and classmates might get hurt.

Introduce the Book

In advance, prepare a book as a model. Define the word *citizen* for children. As you read page 1, use maps to clarify the meanings of the words *community, state,* and *country.* On page 3, explain the difference between rules and laws. As you read, invite children to brainstorm possible responses for each page. Explain that students will create their own books about their own actions.

Make the Book

Distribute copies of the reproducible book pages and assist children as they assemble their own books. As an alternative, provide children with preassembled books. On the cover, invite children to draw a picture of themselves in the center. On page 1, have them fill in the information. For the rest of the book, suggest that children complete the text on each page prior to drawing. Remind them that their illustrations should match the text. Encourage children to include themselves in their illustrations.

Share the Book

Allow opportunities for volunteers to share their books with the class. Examine the variety of responses children have included in their books.

Beyond the Book

- Role-play examples of good citizenship in a variety of community places, such as a store, movie theater, playground, ball field, pool, and library.
- Create a reproducible classmate award and keep copies in a writing center. Invite children to create awards for one another anytime a classmate has demonstrated good citizenship.

Two Views

pages 81–85

Purpose

Children view places from two perspectives: from eye level (front) and from directly overhead (above). Learning about overhead perspective is essential for reading maps.

Strategies for Starting

Provide a variety of objects such as a stuffed animal, plant, apple, desk, globe, lamp, or book. Have children examine the items first from eye level and then from directly above. Ask them to name the features they see from each view. Ask children which view provides the most information about the object.

Introduce the Book

In advance, prepare a book as a model. Read the book aloud to children. On page 2, point out that the view of Tim's house from the front also includes a partial view of the side yards. The overhead view on page 3 shows Tim's entire yard and the things in it. Invite children to compare the two views and note what they can see in each. Ask how the views are similar and different. Discuss the map on page 8. Compare it to the drawings on pages 6 and 7.

Make the Book

Distribute copies of the reproducible book pages

and assist children as they assemble their own books. As an alternative, provide children with preassembled books. Explain that there are many choices for filling in the blanks on each page with things that they can see. Encourage them to note the different things each view allows them to see.

Share the Book

Invite children to read their completed books with a partner. Encourage them to compare and contrast their answers.

Beyond the Book

- Have children draw maps of their desktop, a construction of blocks, or an arrangement of dollhouse furniture that they can view from above.
- Invite children to imagine what a bird's-eye view of their classroom would look like, and have them draw a picture of it.
- Make a set of cards showing objects from overhead and another set showing the same objects from the front. Invite children to play a game of concentration, matching pairs of cards.

Maps Show Places

pages 86–90

Maps Show Places

by _____

Purpose

Children learn that maps are drawings of places, that they use symbols to stand for objects, and that they can be used to find the relative and geographic location of places and things.

Strategies for Starting

Invite volunteers to draw simple pictures of a house, tree, road, and sidewalk. Point out that the pictures they drew stand for real things. Next, ask volunteers to name the first thing that comes to mind when they hear the names of these community places: fire station, post office, toy store, grocery store, or hardware store. Explain that the things they named could be drawn as

symbols for these places. Tell children that they will be learning about small pictures called symbols and how symbols are used on maps. Invite children to share prior knowledge about maps and how they are used.

Introduce the Book

In advance, prepare a book as a model. As you read, pause on the individual pages to discuss the features of the maps shown. Explain that the maps on pages 2, 4, and 6 use symbols to stand for objects or places. These symbols appear in a map key. Identify the symbols on each map. Using the map on page 6, practice locating various places in Sunny City.

Make the Book

Distribute copies of the reproducible book pages and assist children as they assemble their own books. As an alternative, provide children with preassembled books. Explain to children that they will fill in the missing information on each page using the information shown on the maps. On page 8, children will draw their own simple map. (If they need more space, have them use the inside back cover.) Show them where to write the map title and where to draw the symbols in the map key. You might provide suggestions of places to map, such as a school playground, a classroom, or a room in their homes.

Share the Book

Provide opportunities for children to read their completed books with a partner. Invite children to share their maps on page 8 with the class.

Beyond the Book

- Have children use words and phrases such as *next to, to the right of, to the left of, behind, on, between, near,* and *far* to compare the locations of things in your classroom.
- Make a "Maps Show Places" display using the maps on page 8 of the completed books.
- Make an oversized floor plan map of your school on mural paper. Invite children to design symbols to stand for each room. Have them use the map to practice naming relative locations and describing routes to get from one place to another.

Directions Show Which Way

pages 91–95

Directions Show Which Way
by _____

Purpose

Children learn to recognize and use cardinal directions: north, east, south, and west. They also learn to use cardinal directions to locate places and objects on maps.

Strategies for Starting

On a globe, locate the North Pole, South Pole, and equator. Explain to children that the North Pole is the northernmost place on Earth and the South Pole is the southernmost place. Point out that both poles are the coldest locations on Earth. Tell students that the equator is an imaginary line around Earth that lies halfway between the poles. Explain that areas near the equator are the hottest places on the planet.

Introduce the Book

In advance, prepare a book as a model. Refer to a classroom globe as you read aloud pages 1 and 2 to children. Name and point to the directional arrows on pages 1 and 2. Have children stand and form a human compass as in the illustration on page 2. Continue reading aloud the book, pausing to explain how you determined each answer using the information provided in the illustrations.

Make the Book

Distribute copies of the reproducible book pages and assist children as they assemble their own books. As an alternative, provide children with preassembled books. You might have children complete their books as a small-group or whole-group activity so that you can provide guidance. Explain that children will look at the illustration on each page to determine the text they will fill in. On page 7, you might have children color the squares they land on after following each step in the directions.

Share the Book

Provide opportunities for small groups of children to take turns reading their completed books together. All responses on pages 2–7 should be the same. Encourage the groups to use cardinal directions to name the location of additional things and places in the illustrations or in maps.

Beyond the Book

- Use a compass to identify true north in your classroom and then label the walls with the directions north, east, south, and west. Have children stand in a clear area in the center of the room. Give directions such as:

  Pretend you're a penguin and waddle south to the South Pole.

  Pretend you're a whale and swim west to the Pacific Ocean.

- Label your classroom walls with cardinal directions. Then have children play hide-and-seek using an object. Ask volunteers to hide an object and give directional clues to their classmates to find it.

TEACHING TIP: Knowledge of left and right is helpful when learning about the cardinal directions of west and east. Provide opportunities for children to practice using left and right. You might play a game of Simon Says or dance the "Hokey Pokey" to reinforce these concepts.

Home, Sweet Home

by _____

What else do you know about homes?
Draw a picture and write about it.

senior residence

houseboat

house

mobile home

apartment building

There are many kinds of _____

2

Homes give us shelter.

Homes give us a place to _____

1

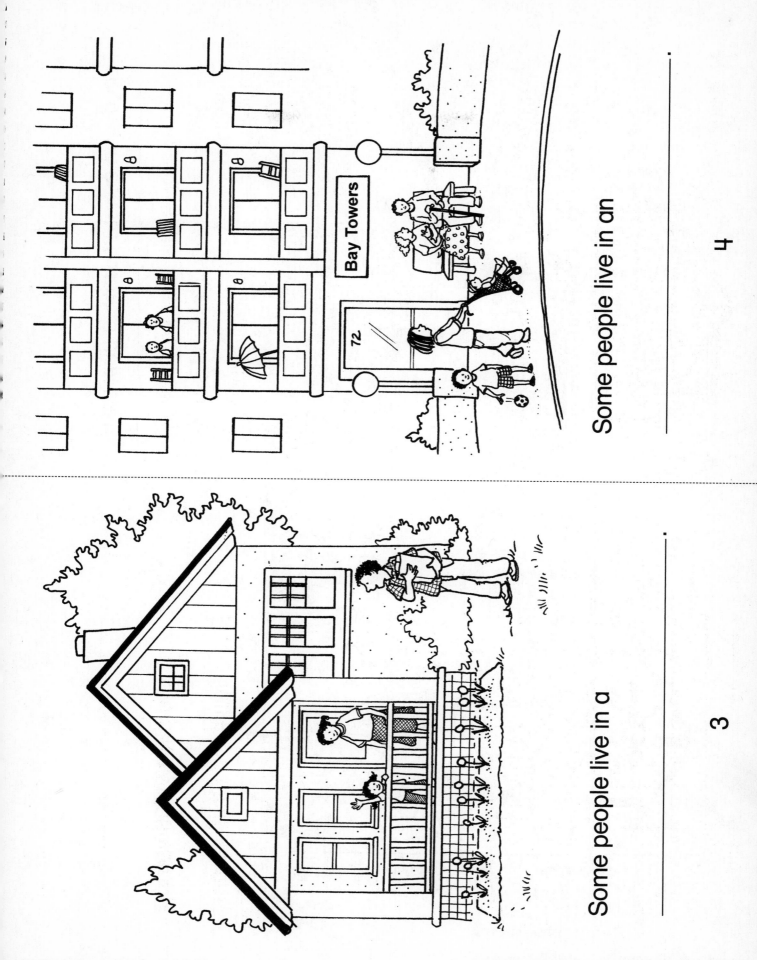

Some people live in an

4

Some people live in a

3

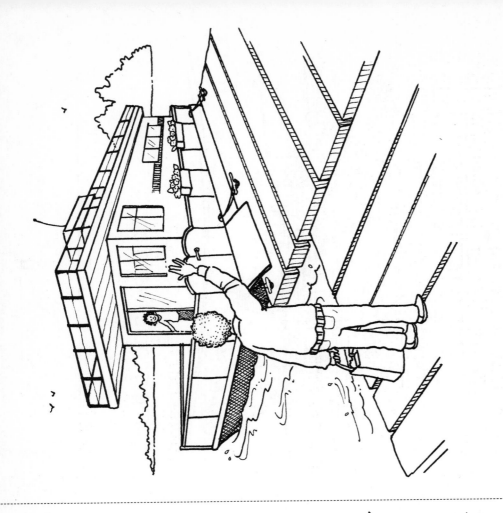

Some people live on a

This kind of home moves on water.

6

Some people live in a

5

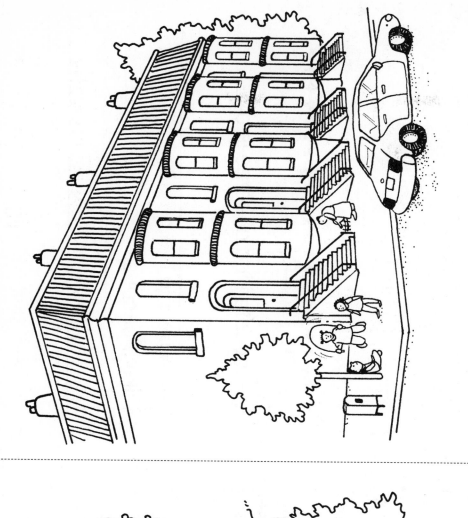

Homes can be near or far from
each other.

These homes are ———
each other.

8

Some people live in a
———.

This kind of home moves on land.

7

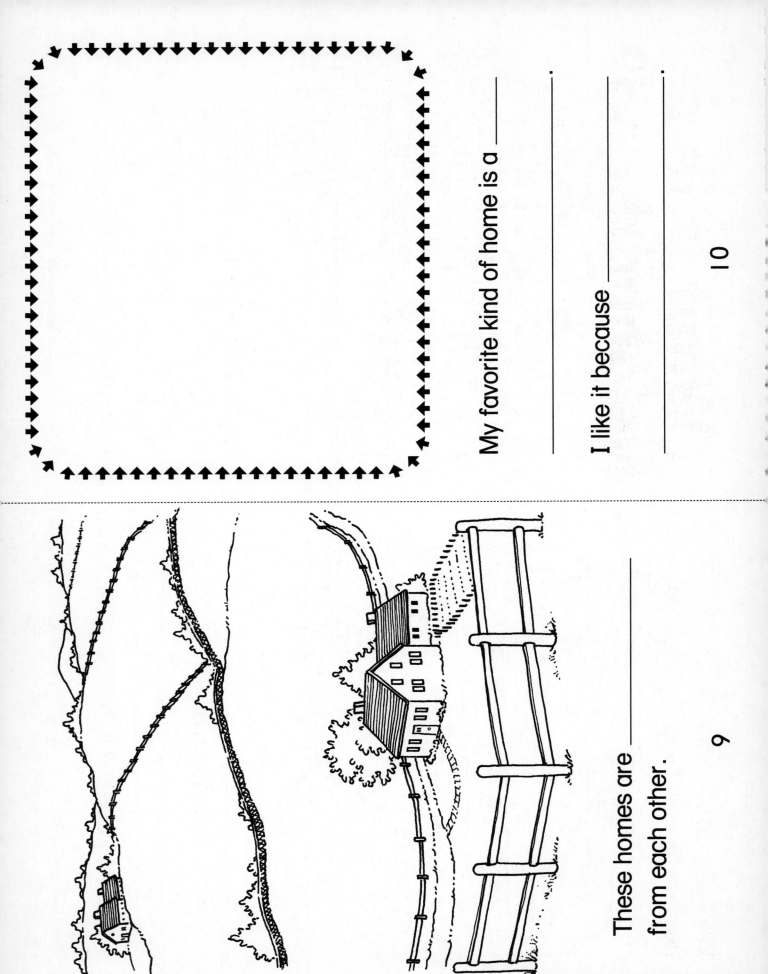

My favorite kind of home is a _____

_____

I like it because _____

_____

10

These homes are _____
from each other.

9

What Is in a Neighborhood?

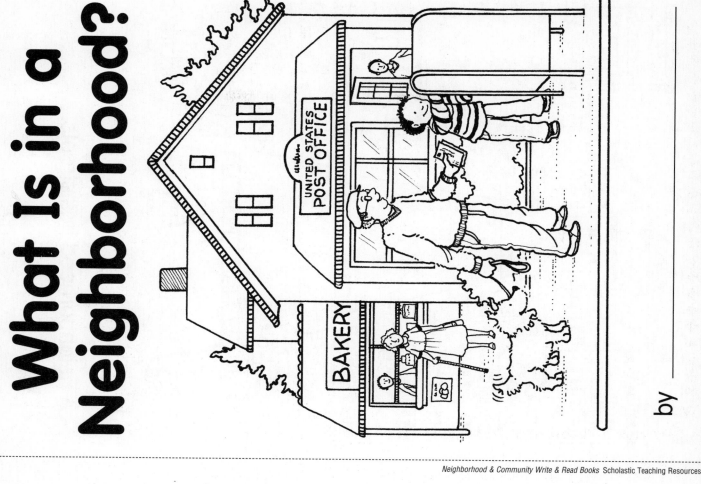

by _____

What else do you know about neighborhoods? Draw a picture and write about it.

_____

_____

_____

_____

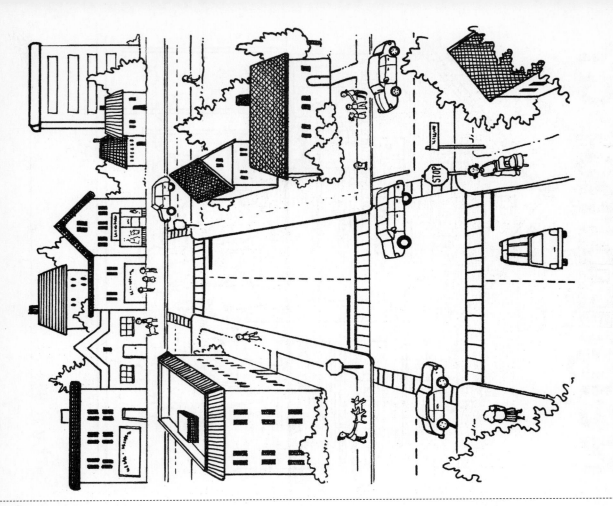

A neighborhood has streets.

2

Your neighborhood is the area around your home.

1

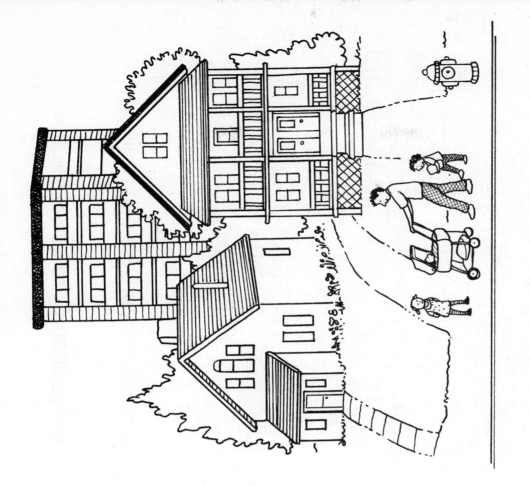

A neighborhood has places to live.

4

My favorite street is _____

I like this street because _____
_____.

3

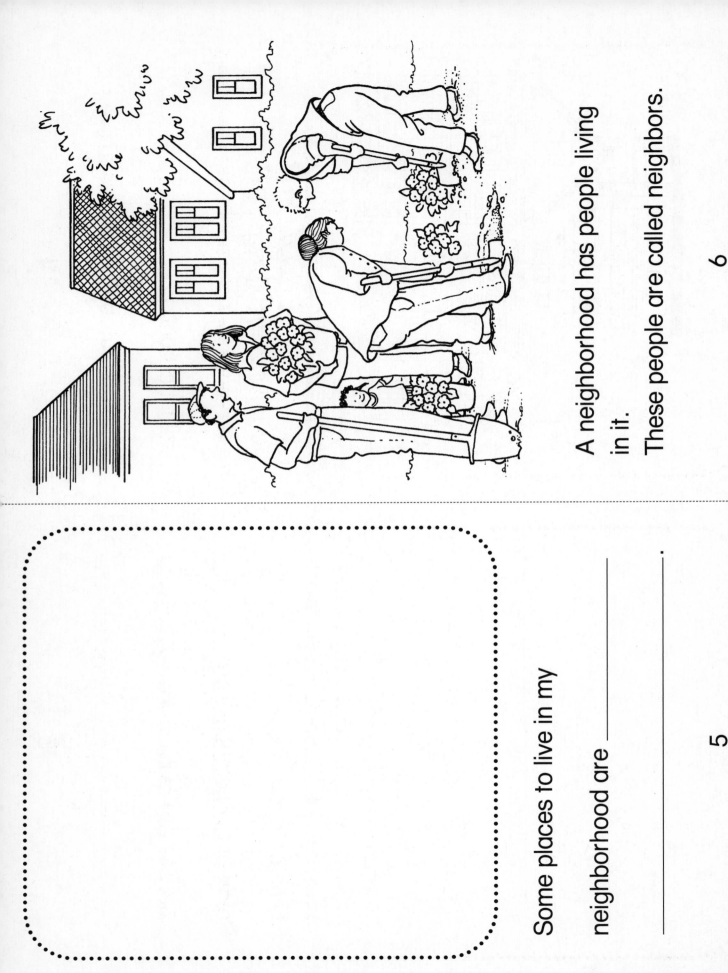

A neighborhood has people living
in it.
These people are called neighbors.

6

Some places to live in my

neighborhood are _____

_____.

5

All neighborhoods are different.
Something special about my

neighborhood is _____

_____.

8

Some of my neighbors are _____

_____

_____.

7

Communities Big and Small

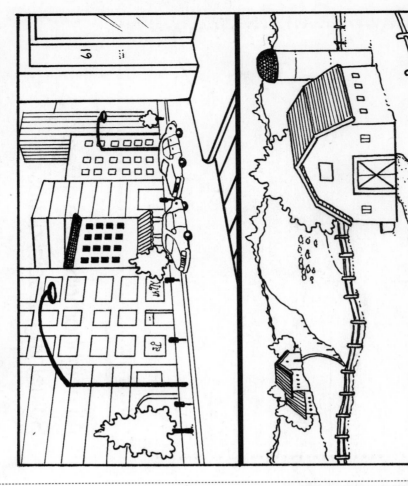

by _____

Neighborhood & Community Write & Read Books Scholastic Teaching Resources

What else do you know about communities? Draw a picture and write about it.

Communities have places to _____

_____

2

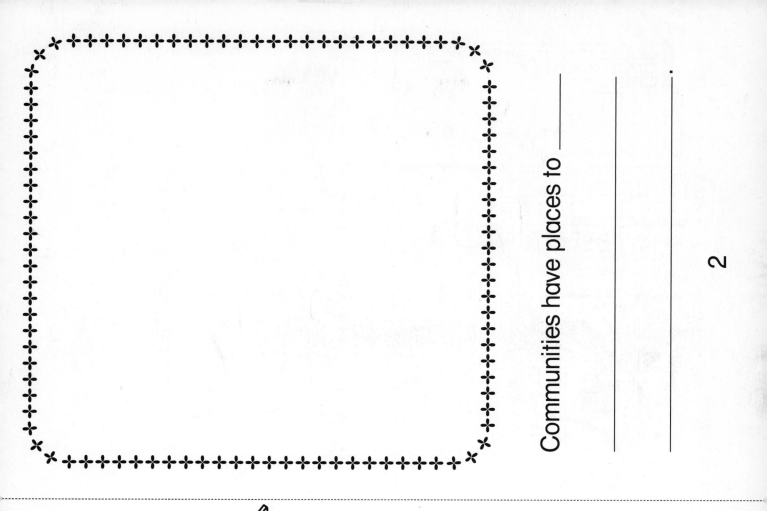

Welcome
to
Seaside

A community is a group.
of neighborhoods.
Each community has a name.

1

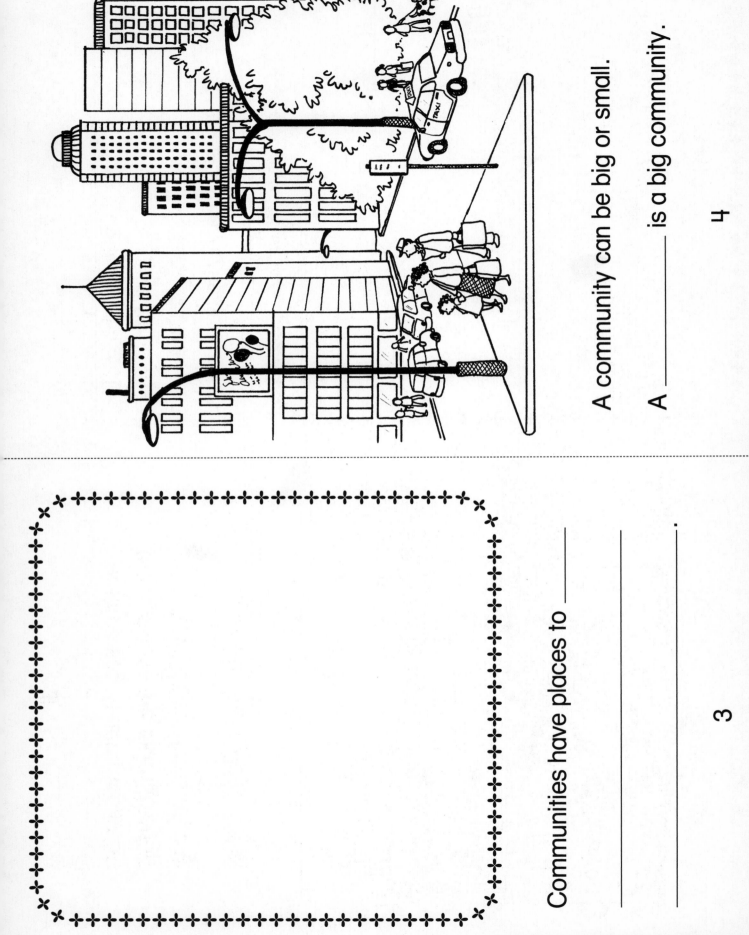

A community can be big or small.

A ＿＿＿＿＿ is a big community.

4

Communities have places to ＿＿＿＿＿

＿＿＿＿＿＿＿＿＿＿

＿＿＿＿＿＿＿＿＿＿ .

3

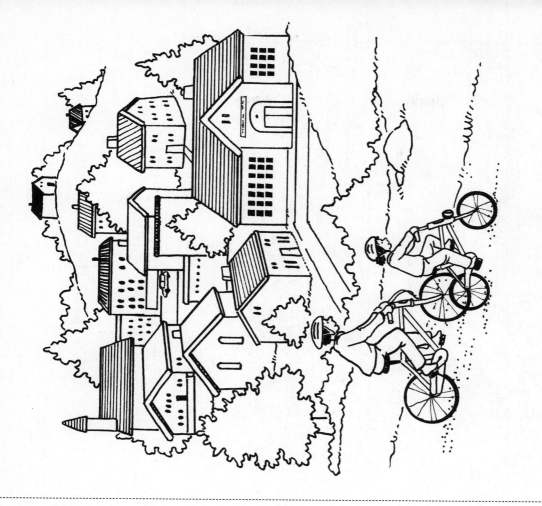

A town is another kind
of community.
It is smaller than a city.

6

Many people live and work

in a _____.
Some people live in apartment
buildings.

5

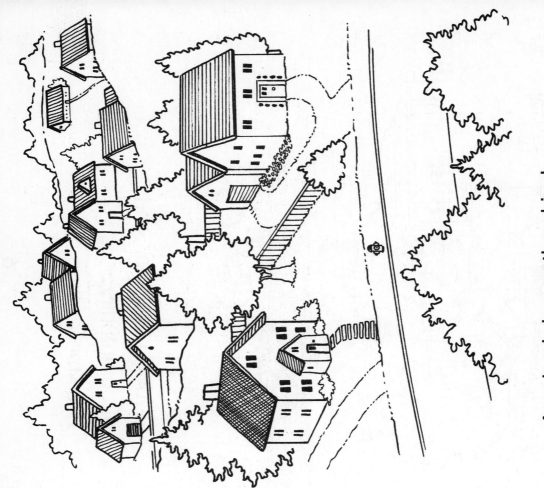

A suburb is another kind
of community.
Suburbs have many homes.

8

Some towns have a main street.

Along the street are _____

and _____.

7

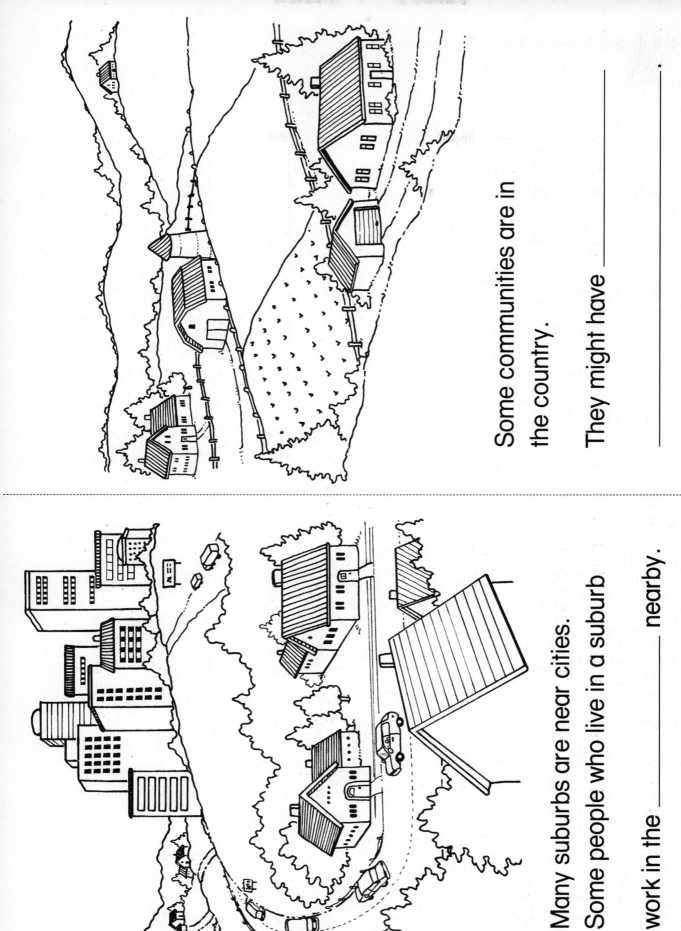

Some communities are in
the country.

They might have _____

_____ .

10

Many suburbs are near cities.
Some people who live in a suburb

work in the _____ _____ nearby.

9

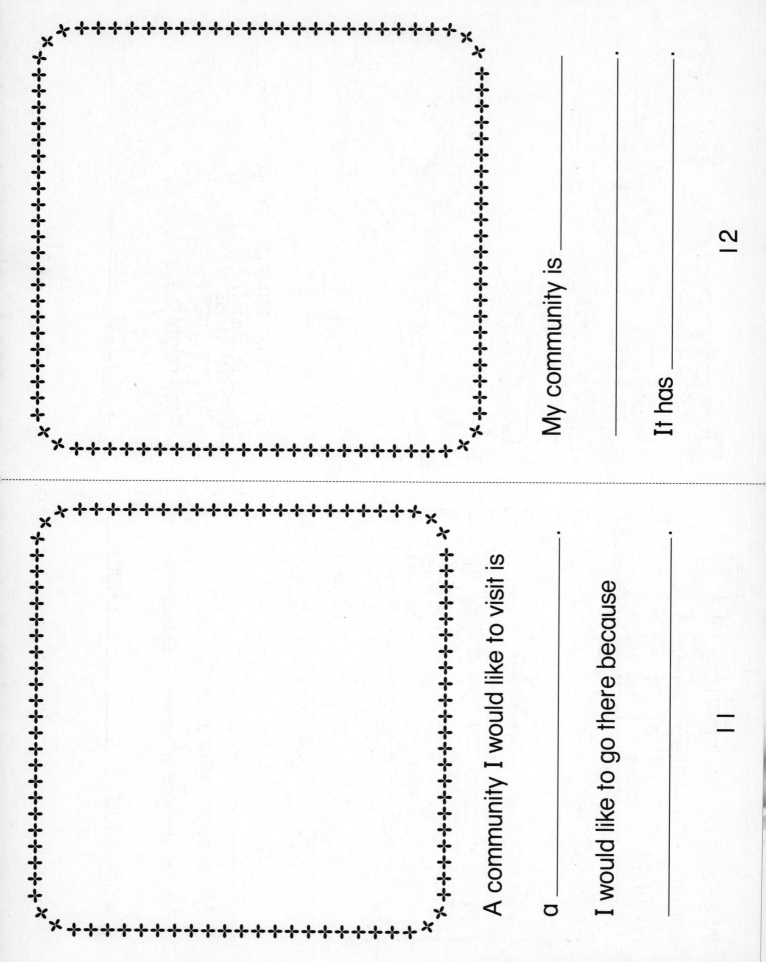

My community is

_____.

It has

_____.

12

A community I would like to visit is

a _____.

I would like to go there because

_____.

11

Postcards From the Country

Dear Grandma,
We are having
a wonderful time!

by _____

What else do you know about the country? Draw a picture and write about it.

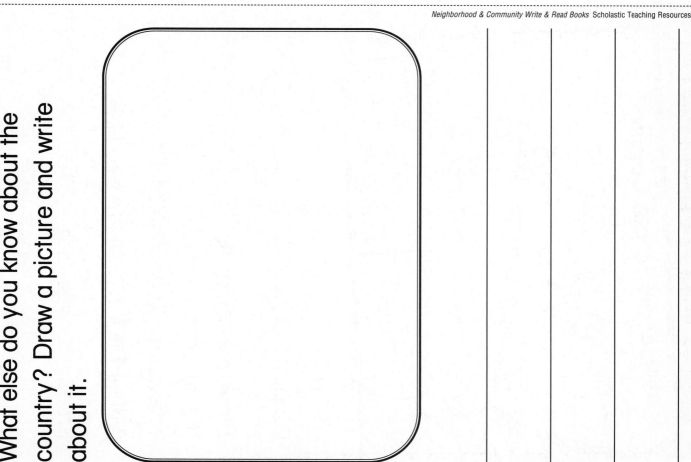

Country Farms

Dear _____,

There are farms in the country.
Farmers grow food to eat.

They grow _____

and _____.

From, _____

2

Welcome to the Country!

Dear _____,

I'm in the country!
It is far from the city.
There are wide-open spaces
of land here.

From, _____

1

Perfect Picks

Dear _____,

There are orchards in the country.

The orchards have fruit trees.

The fruit trees grow _____

and _____.

From, _____

4

Rural Ranches

Dear _____,

There are ranches in the country.

People raise animals on ranches.

They raise _____

and _____.

From, _____

3

Wild Woodlands

Dear _____,

There are forests in the country.

Forests have tall _____.

Some forest animals are _____ _____.

From, _____

6

Hot Spots

Dear _____,

There are deserts in the country.
Deserts are dry and sandy places.

In the desert there are _____ _____.

From, _____

5

Greetings From

_____

Dear _____,

This place is a _____.

There are _____.

From, _____

8

Mighty Mountains

Dear _____,

There are mountains in the country.
Mountains are very high land.

People _____ in the mountains.

From, _____

7

A City Walk

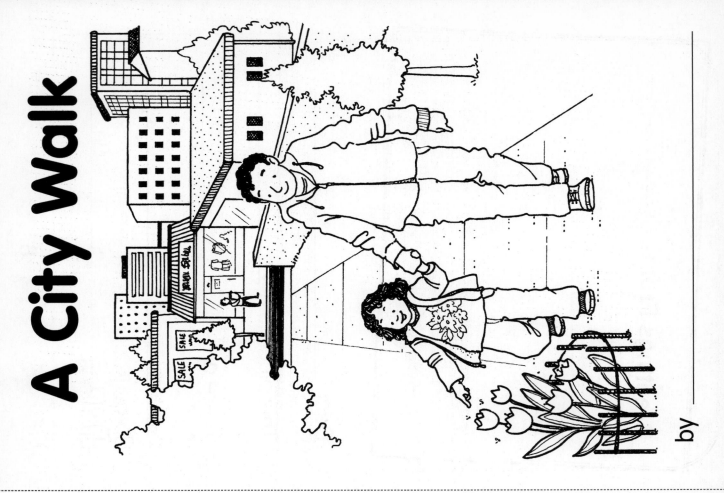

by _____

What else do you know about cities?
Draw a picture and write about it.

I see tall _____.

Some people work in these buildings.

Let's take a walk around the city!
What do you see?

I see ———————— .
They help people move from place
to place.

3

I see ———————— .
They sell many different things.

4

I see _____

This is where visitors can stay overnight.

6

I see _____

This is where some people live.

5

I see places to visit, like

_____

and _____ .

7

If I visited a city, I would like to

_____

_____ .

8

I Travel

by _____

Neighborhood & Community Write & Read Books Scholastic Teaching Resources

What else do you know about transportation? Draw a picture and write about it.

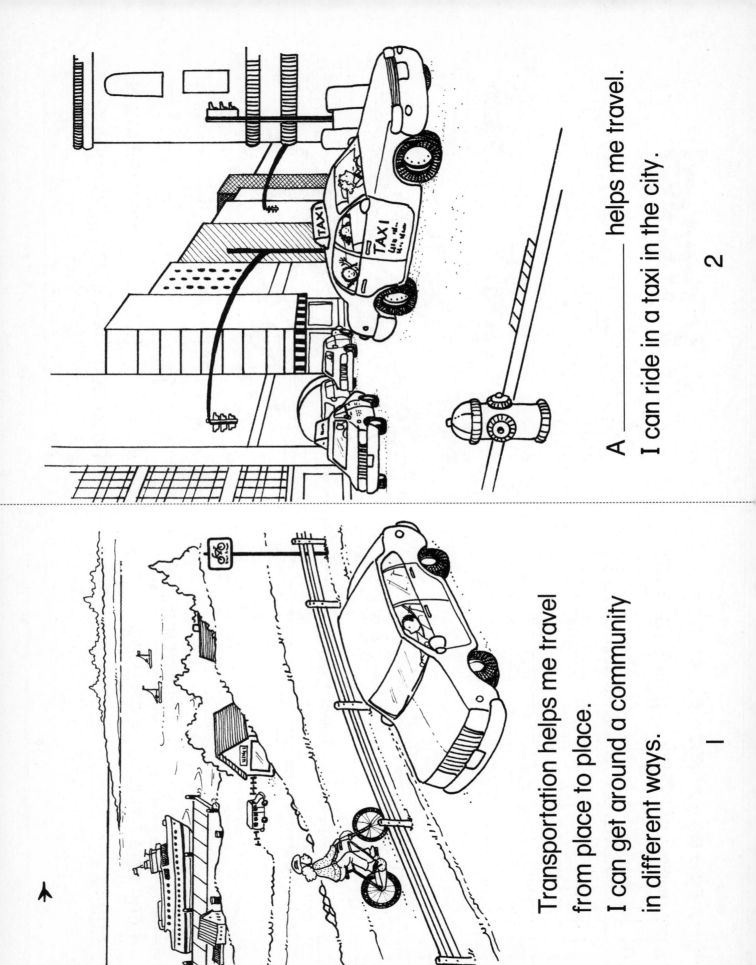

A _____ helps me travel.

I can ride in a taxi in the city.

2

Transportation helps me travel
from place to place.
I can get around a community
in different ways.

1

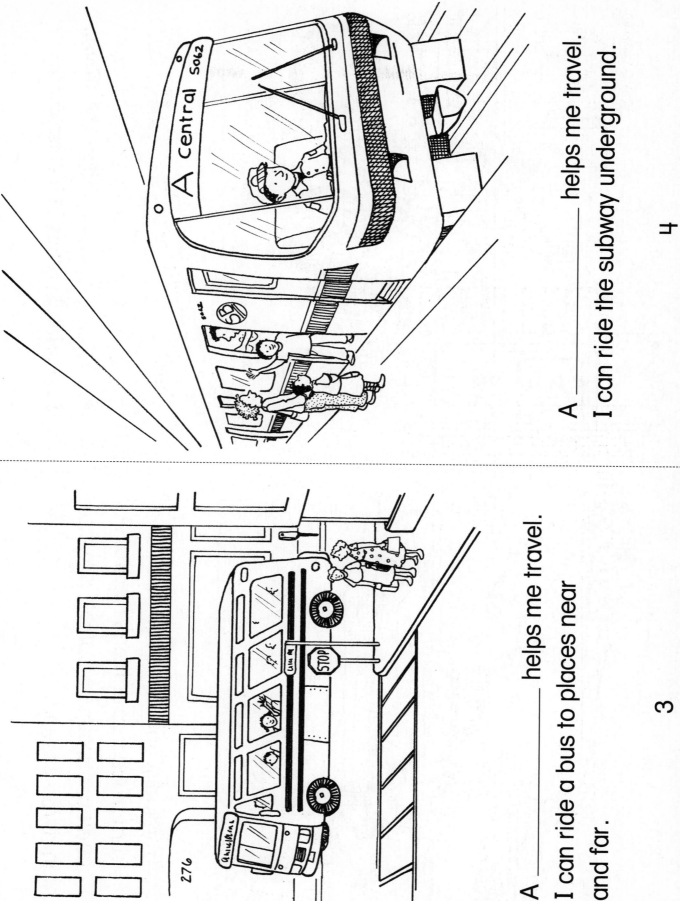

A _____ helps me travel.

I can ride the subway underground.

4

A _____ helps me travel.

I can ride a bus to places near
and far.

3

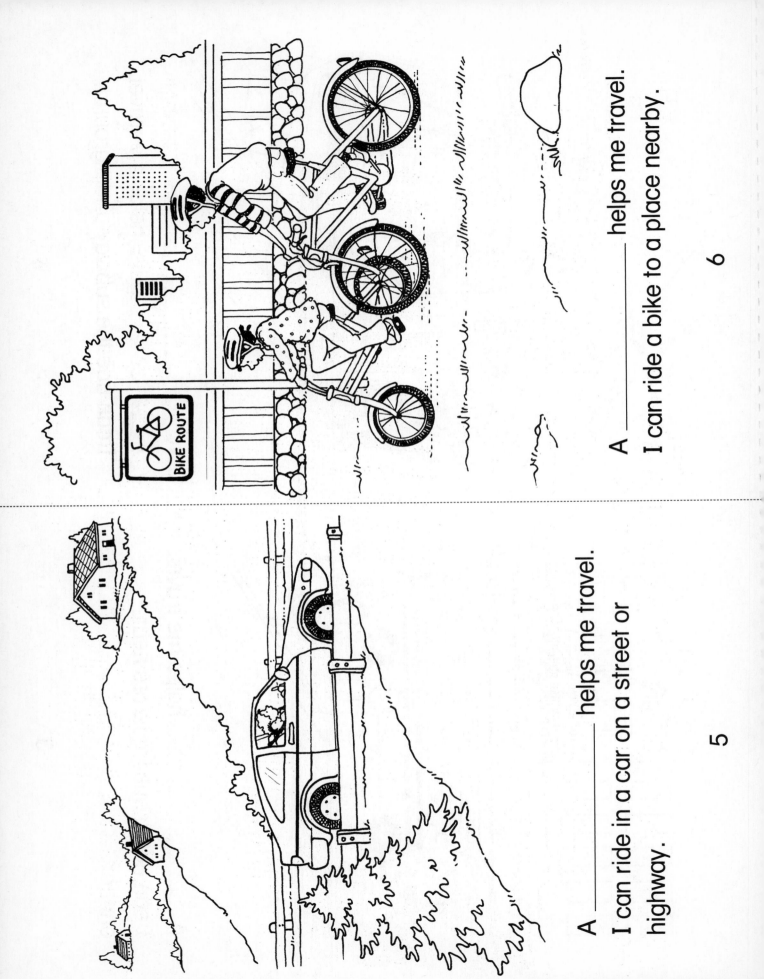

A _____ helps me travel.

I can ride a bike to a place nearby.

6

A _____ helps me travel.

I can ride in a car on a street or highway.

5

A _____ helps me travel.
I can ride on a plane to communities far away!

8

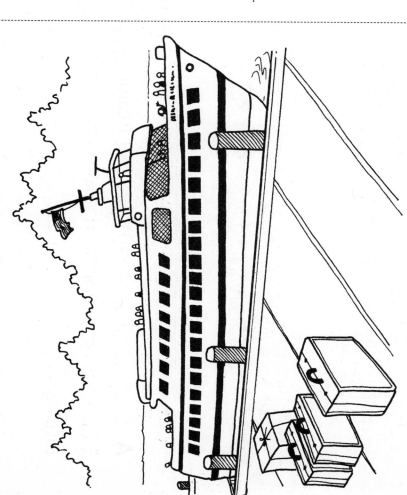

A _____ helps me travel.
I can ride in a boat to cross the water.

7

Community Signs

by _____

What else do you know about community signs?

Draw a picture and write about it.

_____

_____

_____

Signs can help me find things.
This sign tells me where to find a

2

I like to read community signs.
Signs help me all the time.

1

These signs tell me where to find a

_____.

I would use the restroom on the

_____.

4

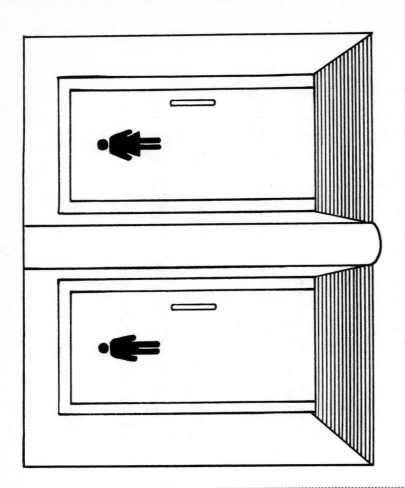

This sign tells me where to find a

_____.

3

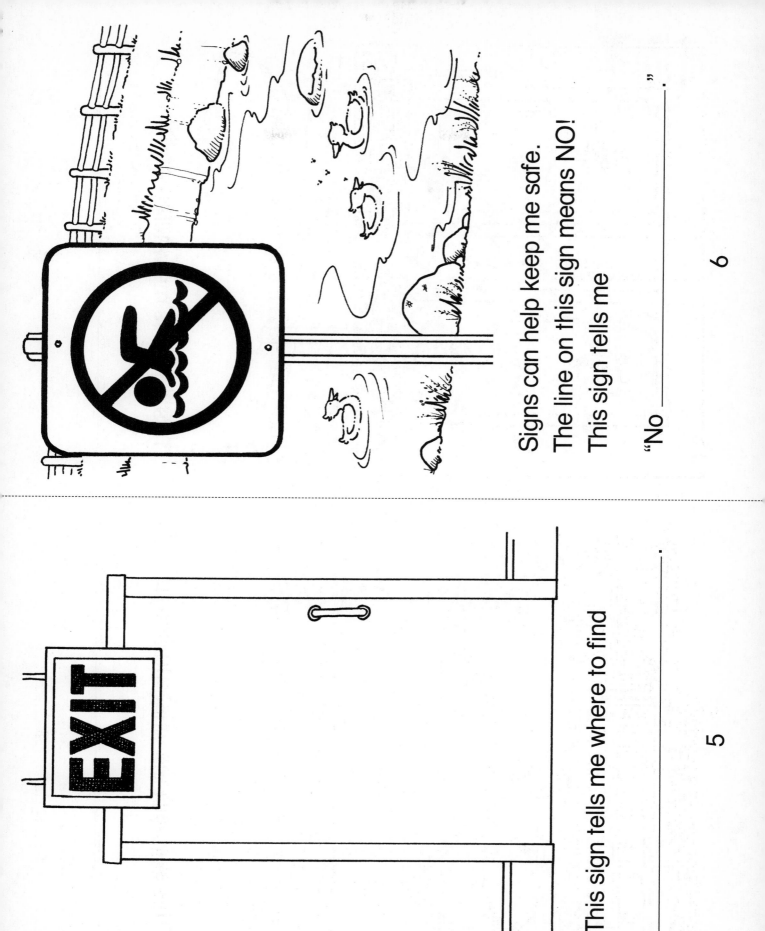

Signs can help keep me safe.
The line on this sign means NO!
This sign tells me

"No _____."

6

This sign tells me where to find

_____.

5

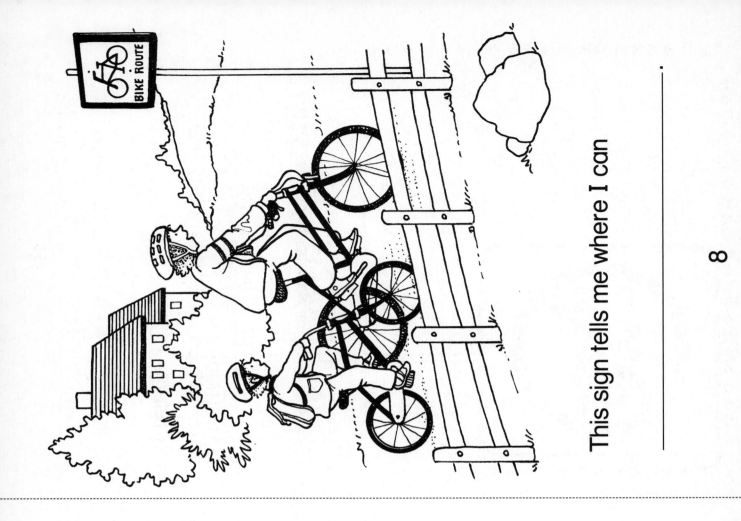

This sign tells me where I can _____.

8

This sign tells me when I can _____.

7

This is another sign in my community.

It tells me _____
_____.

10

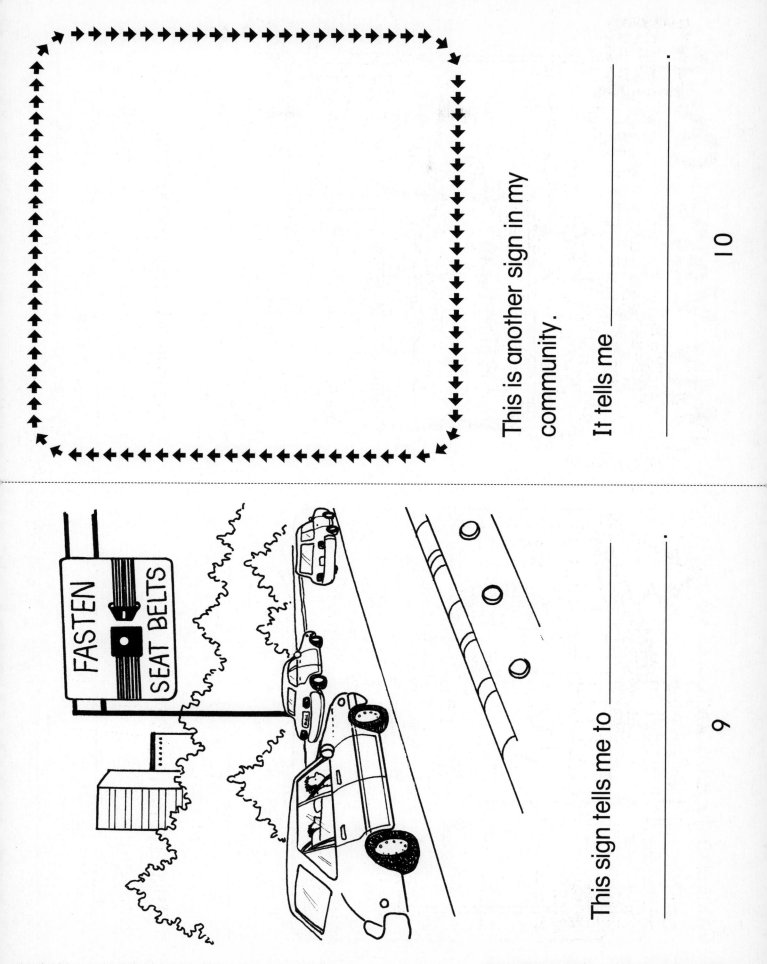

This sign tells me to _____
_____.

9

My Very Own Community

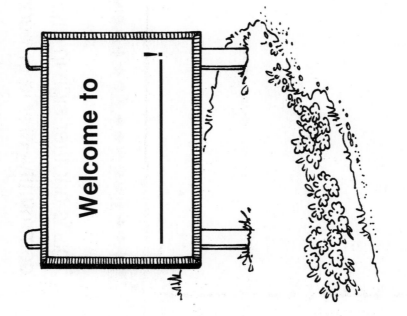

Welcome to
_____!

by _____

Neighborhood & Community Write & Read Books Scholastic Teaching Resources

What else do you know about your community? Draw a picture and write about it.

The land in my community is

_____.

A body of water in or near my

community is _____.

2

The name of my community is

_____.

It is a _____.

(type of community)

1

My community has places to shop.

One place to shop is _____ .

4

My community has places to live.

One place to live is _____ .

3

My community has places to learn.

One place to learn is _____

_____.

6

My community has places to play.

One place to play is _____

_____.

5

My community has places to visit.

One place to visit is _____ _____.

8

My community has places to work.

One place to work is _____ _____.

7

My community has different kinds of transportation.

One way to travel is _____

_____.

9

I like my community because

_____

_____.

10

Meet Community Helpers

by _____

Neighborhood & Community Write & Read Books Scholastic Teaching Resources

What else do you know about community helpers? Draw a picture and write about it.

A crossing guard helps people

_____

_____.

2

All communities have workers.
The jobs they do help people.

1

A librarian helps people

_____

4

A teacher helps people

_____

3

A firefighter helps people

_____

_____

6

A bus driver helps people

_____

_____

5

Another community helper I know is

_____ .

This person helps me

_____

8

A police officer helps people

_____ .

7

What Do They Do?

by _____

What else do you know about other jobs people have? Draw a picture and write about it.

Tailor! Tailor!
What do you do?

I am sewing ———
just for you!

2

Baker! Baker!
What do you do?

I am baking ———
just for you!

1

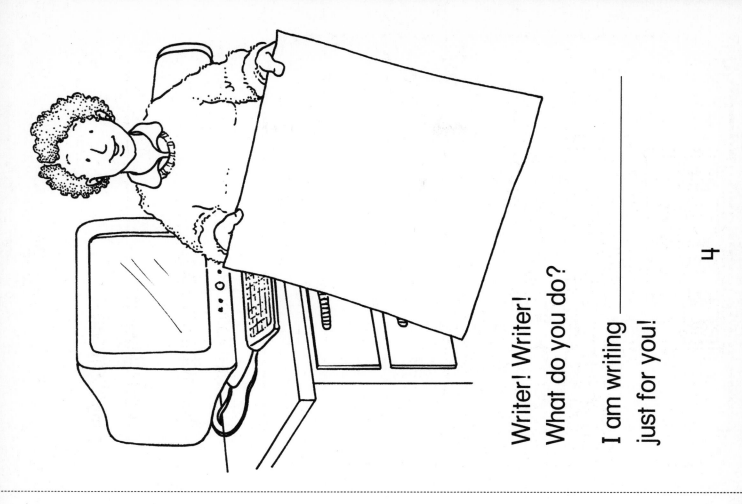

Writer! Writer!
What do you do?

I am writing _____
just for you!

4

Farmer! Farmer!
What do you do?

I am growing _____
just for you!

3

Children! Children!
What will you do?

I would like to be a ———
just like you!

Builder! Builder!
What do you do?

I am building ———
just for you!

Neighborhood & Community Write & Read Books Scholastic Teaching Resources

From Farm to Me

by _____

What else do you know about farms?
Draw a picture and write about it.

2. The farmer plants the seeds.

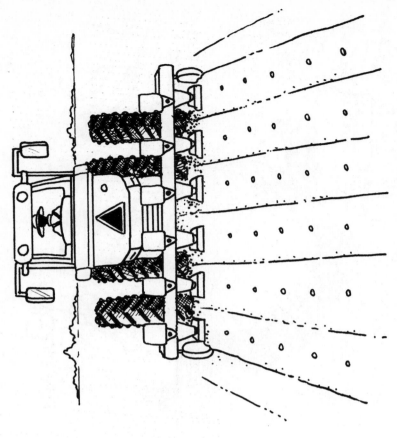

This machine plants ——
in each row.

2

1. The farmer plows the soil.

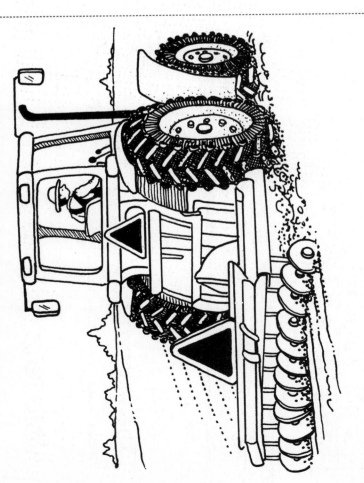

Farmers grow foods that I eat.
Machines help the farmer work.
This machine makes rows in the

.

1

4. The seeds grow into plants.

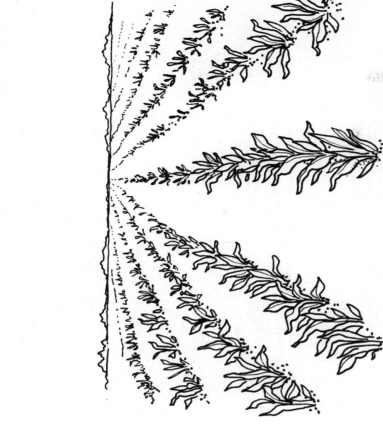

The plants grow vegetables like
_____.

The plants grow fruit like
_____.

4

3. The farmer waters the seeds.

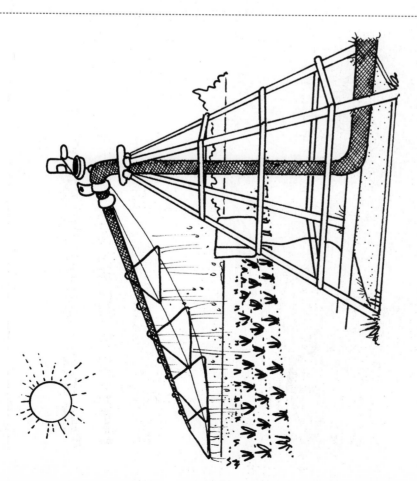

This machine gives the seeds
_____.

Water helps the seeds grow.

3

6. Trucks move the crop.

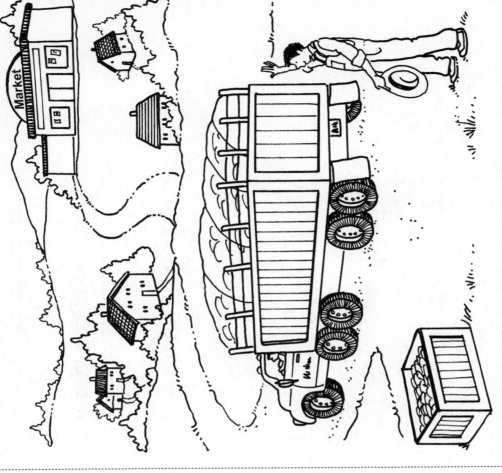

Trucks carry the crops to

_____.

6

5. The farmer picks the crop.

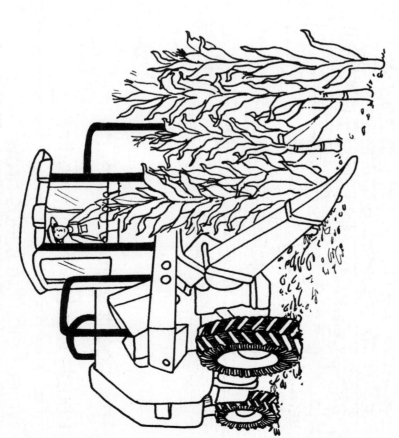

The crop is ready.
This machine helps the farmer

_____.

5

8. We eat the food!

A vegetable I like is

A fruit I like is

8

---

7. Stores sell the crops.

GREEN LETTUCE

SWEET CORN

SUMMER SQUASH

GREEN BEANS

People can buy their favorite

7

I Am a Good Citizen

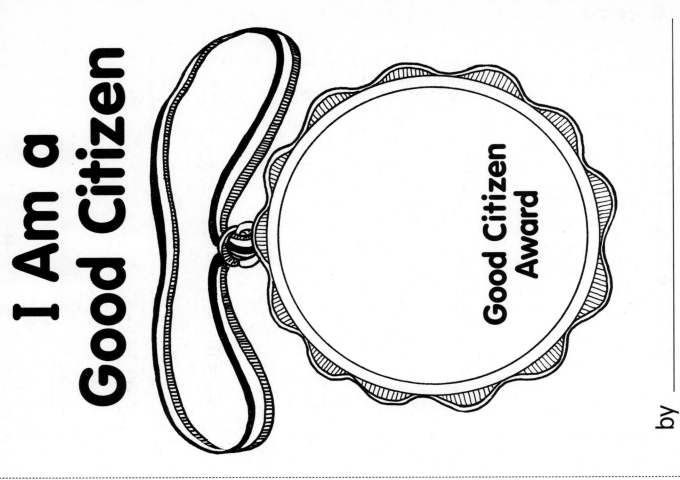

Good Citizen Award

by _____

What else do you know about being a good citizen? Draw a picture and write about it.

Good citizens help others.

I help others when I _____

_____ .

2

My Community:
_____

My State:
_____

My Country:
_____

I am a member of a community,
state, and country.

I am a citizen!

I

Good citizens work with others.

I work with others when I _____ _____.

4

Good citizens follow rules.

One rule I follow is _____ _____.

3

Good citizens solve problems together.
I solve problems when I _____.

6

Good citizens keep the community clean.
I keep the community clean when I _____.

5

Being a good citizen is important

_____

because _____

8

Hooray for good citizens!
We make the world a better place.

7

Two Views

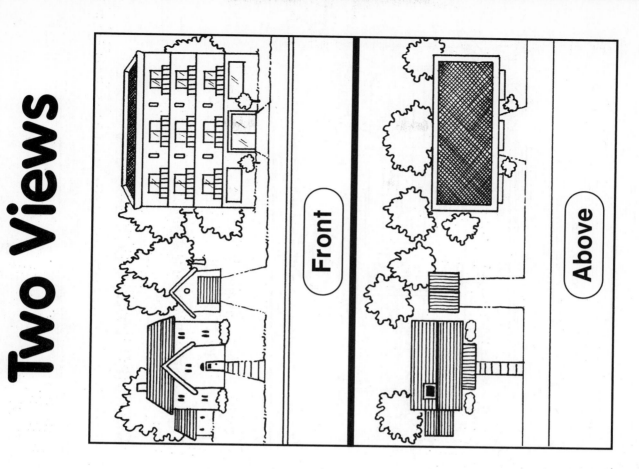

Front

Above

by _____

Draw a picture of something from above.
Then write what your picture shows.

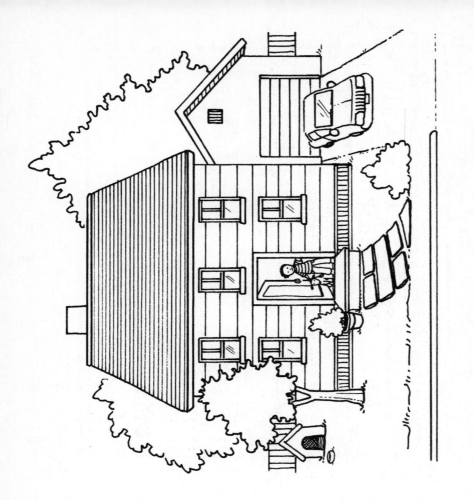

This is the front of Tim's house.
I see Tim at the door.

From this view, I can also see ⸺
⸺⸺⸺⸺⸺⸺⸺ .

2

This is Tim.
Tim is going to show us his home, street, and neighborhood.

1

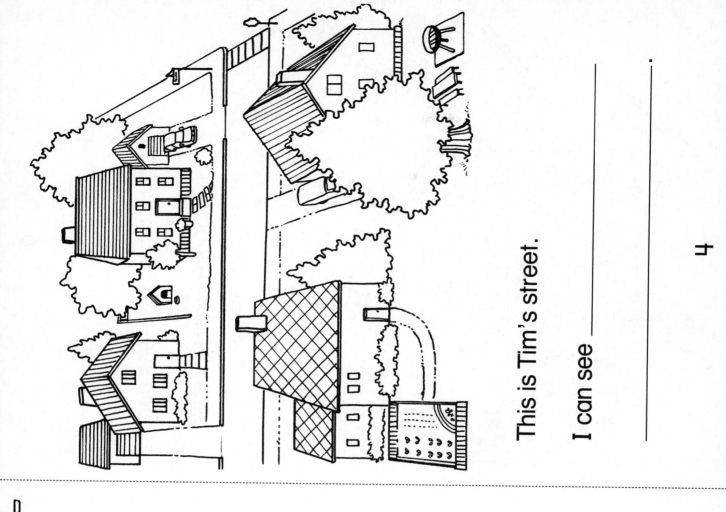

This is Tim's street.

I can see _____.

4

This is Tim's house from above.
I can't see the door.

From this view, I can see _____.

3

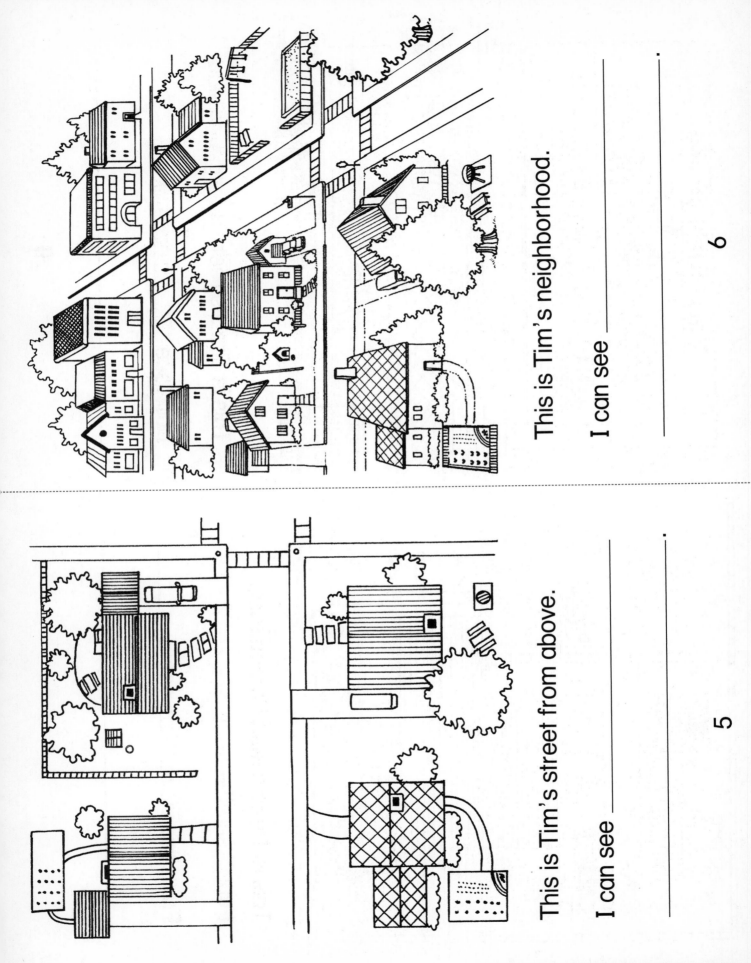

This is Tim's neighborhood.

I can see _____ .

6

This is Tim's street from above.

I can see _____ .

5

Tim's Neighborhood

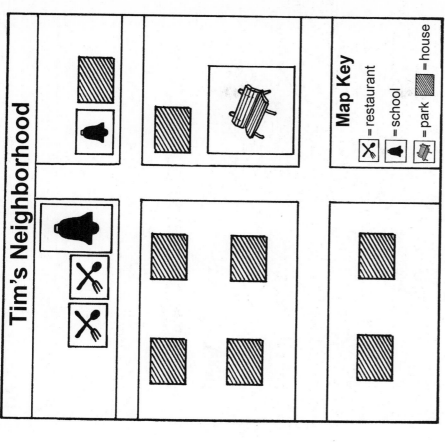

Map Key

✗	= restaurant
🔔	= school
▨	= park
▨	= house

This is a map of Tim's neighborhood.

A map shows a place from _____.

8

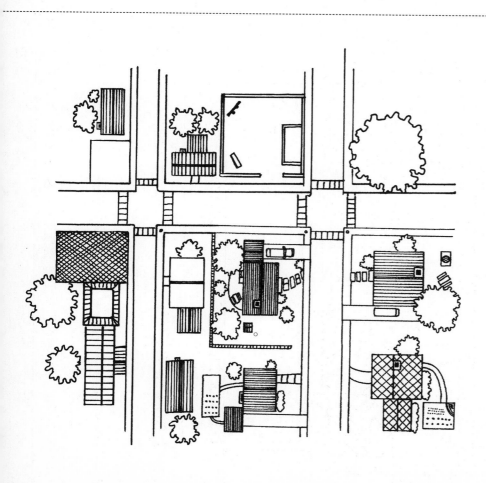

This is Tim's neighborhood from above.

I can see _____.

7

Maps Show Places

by _____

Neighborhood & Community Write & Read Books Scholastic Teaching Resources

What else do you know about maps?
Draw a picture and write about it.

Mr. Hong's Classroom

desk

rug

table

bookshelf

chair

A title tells what the map shows.

This map shows _____

_____

2

A map is a drawing of a place.
It can help you find places.

1

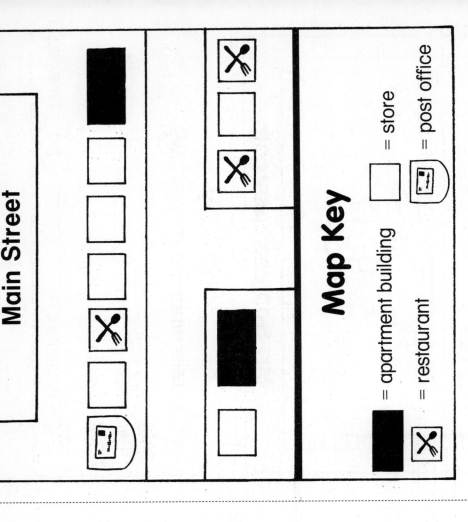

Main Street

Map Key

☐ = apartment building

🍴 = restaurant

☐ = store

📮 = post office

This map shows a different place.

This map shows _____

_____.

4

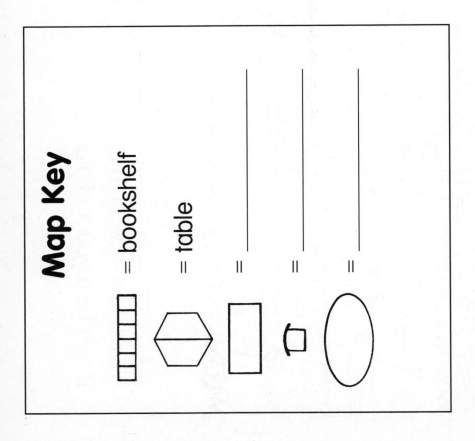

Map Key

▦ = bookshelf

▭ = table

⬡ = _____

▭ = _____

⬭ = _____

Maps show places with drawings
called symbols.
Each symbol stands for something.
Label the symbols above.

3

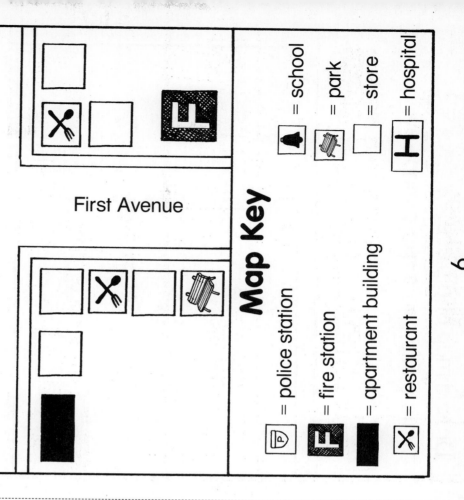

Sunny City

Center Street

First Avenue

H

Map Key

= school

= park

= store

H = hospital

= police station

F = fire station

= apartment building

= restaurant

Look at the map of Main Street.

How many restaurants are there?

_____

How many stores are there?

_____

How many apartment buildings are

there? _____

What is next to the post office?

_____

Draw a map of a place.
Write a title and make a map key.

Map Key

_____ =

_____ =

_____ =

8

Look at the map of Sunny City.

What is next to the hospital?

_____

How many parks are on First

Avenue? _____

On what street is the fire station?

_____

7

Directions Show Which Way

by _____

Neighborhood & Community Write & Read Books Scholastic Teaching Resources

What else do you know about directions?
Draw a picture and write about it.

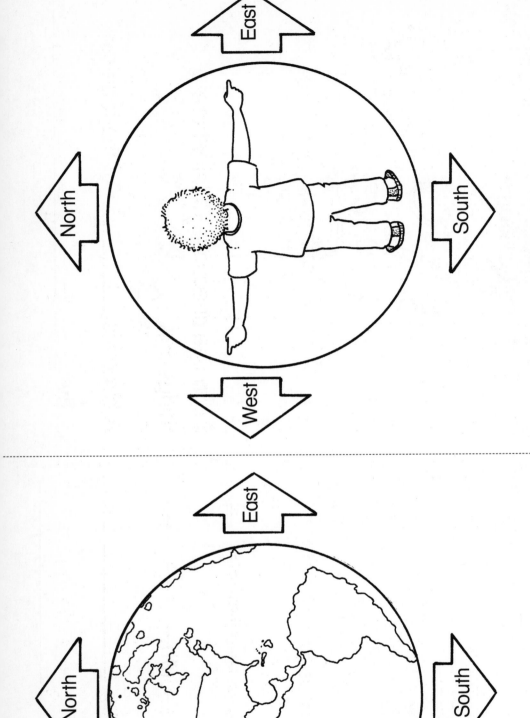

When I face north, south is behind me.

East is to my right.

West is to my _____.

2

North, **east**, **south**, and **west**
are directions.

1

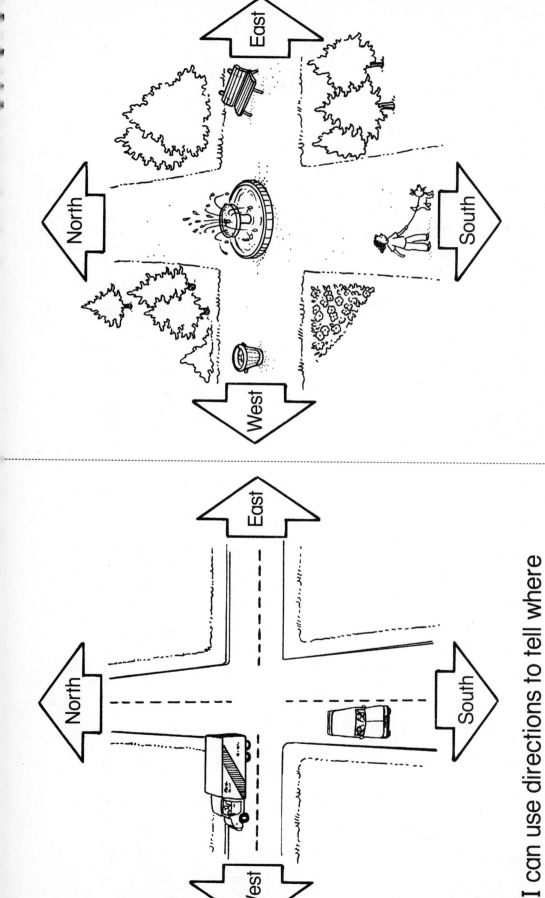

I can use directions to tell where
things are.

A bench is _____ of the fountain.

4

I can use directions to tell where
things are going.

The car is driving south.

The truck is driving _____ .

3

Kama's Bedroom

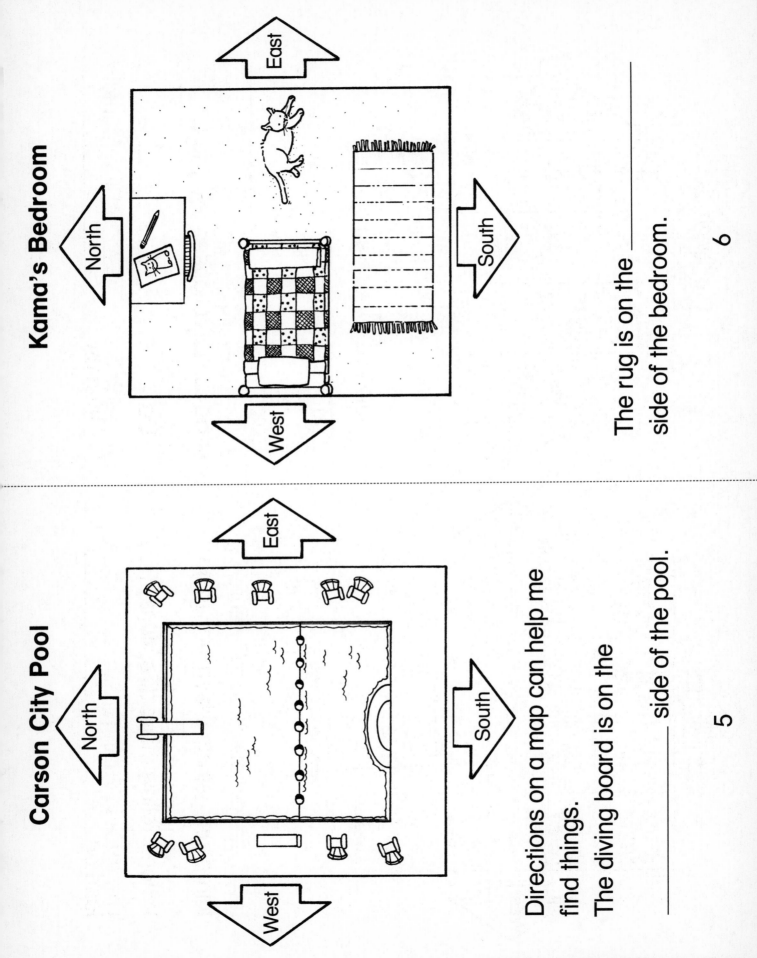

North

East

West

South

The rug is on the _____ side of the bedroom.

6

Carson City Pool

North

East

West

South

Directions on a map can help me find things.

The diving board is on the _____ side of the pool.

5

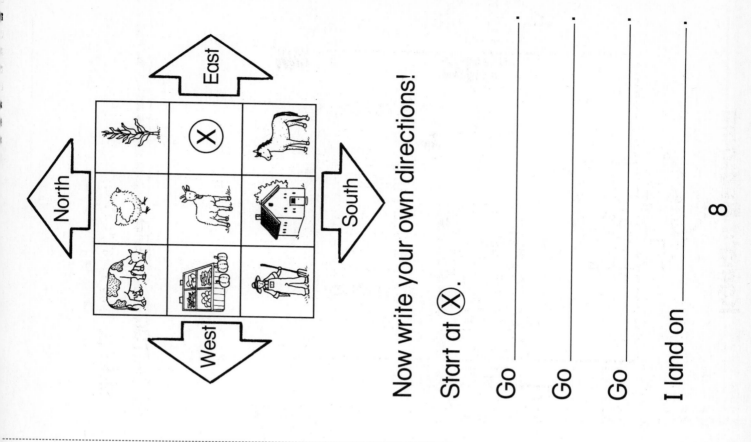

Now write your own directions!

Start at ⊗.

Go _____

Go _____

Go _____

I land on _____ .

8

Start at ⊗.
Go west 2.
Go south 2.
Go east 3.
Go north 3.

Directions tell me which way to go.

When I follow these directions, I

land on _____ .

7

This is a picture of the author,
_____

About the Author

The author of this book is _____
_____ .

_____ is _____ years old

and lives in _____ .

The author likes to _____

_____ , and

_____ .